I0749809

LOOKING BACK

LOOKING BACK

A Memoir

Howard Pollack

Full Court Press
Englewood Cliffs, New Jersey

First Edition

Copyright © 2021 by Howard Pollack

All rights reserved. No part of this book may be reproduced or transmitted in any form or by any means electronic or mechanical, including by photocopying, by recording, or by any information storage and retrieval system, without the express permission of the author, except where permitted by law.

Published in the United States of America
by Full Court Press, 601 Palisade Avenue,
Englewood Cliffs, NJ 07632
fullcourtpress.com

ISBN 978-1-946989-93-2
Library of Congress Control No. 2021909665

Editing and book design by Barry Sheinkopf

Cover photograph, "Curiosity, 1950," by the author

DEDICATION

To my wife, my love, Arlene, and to my parents, sisters, and the children who have been my life.

My photos are rarely posed but capture the life I've lived. The magazines in the background of my father's portrait and the stick in my son's hand capture moments, people, and observations that have given my life its truest meaning.

I am deeply grateful to my beloved friends, Eugenia Koukounas and Barry Sheinkopf, for creating this book as a gift honoring my 90th year on this complex, beautiful earth.

Each aspect of this memoir has as its origin one abiding motif: love.

TABLE OF CONTENTS

LOOKING BACK

STORIES

PHOTOGRAPHS

"Life is not a rehearsal."

—*Howard Pollack*

Looking Back

A MEMOIR

Chapter 1

Exodus to the New World

On May 31, 1898, my father, Abraham Pollak (*sic*) arrived at New York from Rotterdam on the steamer *Spaarndam*, according to Immigration records.

He was 7 years old, accompanied by his mother, Chane, 40 years old, and his siblings: Jacob (9), Esther (8), Eidel (6), and Rivka (6 months). They had a total of eight dollars. My grandfather, Mechel, met them and took them to his residence at 35 Gross Street, Boston.

My father's recollection of the voyage, in steerage, was ghastly. He remembered eating dates torn from a huge block, sticky and bug-infested, and, after days at sea, nauseating. Till the day he died, this image kept him from ever again eating dates.

He remembered the dock in Rotterdam where the family had

gathered to board. Rivka was holding a cup of milk given to her by a kind Dutch person. Passersby dropped coins into it.

I don't know when Mechel arrived in the U.S., but I do know that he had been a cobbler on a baron's estate in Chorostkow, in what was then Poland. My father's family had lived in a *shtetl* there. He remembered jumping off the horse-drawn wagon filled with kids and cutting *cheder*, religious school, to spend the afternoon in the baron's orchard. By swapping with a peasant slices of white bread that his mom had baked (considered a delicacy, since most peasants ate a heavy, dark bread), the peasant in return gave him free run of the fruit trees. When it was time to go home, he would hop on the wagon returning from *cheder* and make his way back to the *shtetl*—a trick that got him the title "Pollack's Tramp."

He arrived in Boston speaking only Yiddish, since Jews could not attend the Polish schools and learn any other languages. One day, as he was playing on the street in Boston, he was excited to see a fire engine racing to a fire, horns blowing, bells ringing, pulled by a double team of galloping white horses.

He ran after the fire engine and soon found himself lost in the maze of Boston streets. He cried for help in a language that no Boston cop could speak. He was vague about the details of how he finally got home, but thankfully he did.

He went to Boston public schools until the sixth grade and then had to work, selling newspapers on the Boston Commons.

He was a member of the Newsboy's Union and knew Paul Dudley White, a fellow newsboy, who later became a prominent heart surgeon.

While he was known to friends as "Abe," or "Al," for the rest of his life, to me he was always "Pop" or "Papa."

At some time in his early youth, Abe became an apprentice to an uncle who was a plumber, a trade he was to work at until the 1940s.

I never knew my paternal grandparents.

MY MOTHER, ETTE PORTNOY (LATER ETHEL POTTER), born near Kiel in the Ukraine, was 4 years old when she arrived in New York on the *SS Statendam*, on May 26, 1901, after a ten-day voyage out of Rotterdam. She was accompanied by her mother, Basche Portnoy, age 26, as well as her little sister Sonia (later Sarah), age 11 months. They came from Slatapol (perhaps Zlatapol) and were headed for Providence, Rhode Island, where Basche's husband, my maternal grandfather Gadaliah (Charles) Portnoy, was staying with relatives name Mellion. They had four dollars on their persons when they landed in New York City.

Basche was to have two more children fathered by Gadaliah, Jack and Eva Potter, "Potter" being the immigration official's translation of the surname Portnoy.

The early death of Gadaliah was a severe blow to Basche,

now called Bessie Potter. She had been married at the age of 16 and now was a young widow with four children to support in a foreign land. The well-meaning sympathy of the Mellion family and other friends so humiliated her, however, that the young widow left Providence for New York City.

My mother, Ethel, then age 11 or 12 and the oldest, was removed from school and delivered to an aunt in Fall River, Massachusetts, indentured as a house servant; she never returned to school.

I don't know much about Bessie's life in New York at this time, except that she owned a candy store on the Lower East Side. She fell in love with Max Weich. They lived together and had three children, Francis, Evelyn, and Johnny.

My mom, an adolescent newly arrived from Fall River, was assigned to care for the new brood. She felt uncomfortable around Max, sure he had his eyes on her, so she was careful while in his presence.

Max, a genius of the *lumpenproletariat*, lived with the family. Though the family was in dire poverty, however, Max brought home his own food and didn't share it with the others. He'd use butter on his bread but offer only lard to the rest of the family

One day when Johnny was playing on the street, a girl showed him new skates bought for her by Max, a friend of her mother's. This ended the era of Max, as Bessie showed him the door.

I never knew Max, although he was to make his appearance at intervals for many years after.

During my college years, I was surprised to learn from my aunt Frances that she had no birth certificate and, for that reason, could not get a passport to travel abroad. I don't know if this was also true of Evelyn and Johnny, although Johnny did serve in the army during World War II.

My Hebrew name, Chaim Mechel Pollack, honors my grandfather.

Howard's mother and father, c. 1915

Chapter 2

My Early Years

IN 1928, MOM HAD A GYNECOLOGICAL PROBLEM. Her doctor diagnosed it as a cancerous tumor. She was operated on and told she would no longer be able to bear a child. This came as no shock to my parents, since my mother was in her forties and menopausal.

What a surprise when they found out she was pregnant. My sister Gwen was 13 then, and my sister, Esther was 10. When I arrived on May 26, 1929, they were there to greet me. My aunts and uncles from both sides of the family were happy that I was a boy. I understand the *bris* was standing-room only.

My aunt Esther and uncle Jack lived on the Lower East Side in what my family considered a posh building, with an elevator. Esther took care of me for a period of time after the delivery as Mom recovered from complications. Esther had no children of her own and practically swooned with joy over the experience. The story of my time with her during this period was related to me by her many times over in my formative years.

My aunt and uncle brought me home to Chisholme Street in the East Bronx. While I have no recollection of this place, my sisters do.

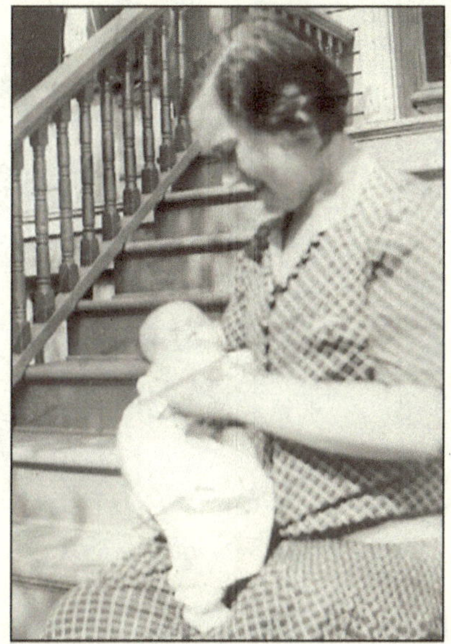

The earliest photo of Howard Pollack

This is a photo of me and my mom, about age 33, holding me on the steps of the house my folks lived in. I must be less than a month old. Herbert Hoover was president. The Great Depression was about to happen.

In a second photo I'm about a year old, surrounded by my parents. The locale was probably Crotona Park in the Bronx. My father, a plumber by trade, would soon be out of work as a result of the Depression.

Howard at about a year old, with his parents

In the third photo, I'm about two. My earliest memories are of that home on Morris Avenue in the Bronx. We lived there until I was four or five. I remember the sandals and clothing I was wearing the day this picture was taken. Notice the pavement I stood on. This was my playground, surrounded by five-story walk-ups. I was standing with my faithful steed, "Cal's Colt," named after our illustrious President Coolidge. The colt

Howard with "Cal's Colt," about age 2

was stabled in the bathtub of our apartment. I can still remember my tantrum the day I discovered my beloved colt had trotted off into the distance and disappeared forever. I realize now that it had been too great a chore for my parents to lift the thing and carry it around.

When I was about two, my pop took me to a nearby fire house, and the fireman let me ring the polished bell on the hook-and-ladder truck. It was a thrill. When the fireman asked my age, I said, "Wait. I'll make it," and held up two fingers, making

Howard with his maternal grandmother

them all laugh.

The neighborhood was teeming with children who used that shared pavement in the photo to skip, run, bounce balls, fence with sticks, shout, sing, and play hide-and-seek. Although we lived on the top floor, five flights up. I was allowed to play in the streets unsupervised, except for the mothers looking out the window from time to time to see what we were up to.

I'd join the mob of kids.

One day I decided to skip down to the candy store and ask the man for a Dixie Cup. I told him I could not pay for it because my father was out of work, but that, as soon as he was working again, the ice cream would be paid for. I don't remember if he actually gave me the ice cream, but he did tell my father, and the incident entered family legend.

It was great fun for us kids to run into the alleys and through the dark building basements replete with piles of coal and odorous garbage cans. In the winter, we'd warm ourselves at the glowing furnaces and watch the super throw shovelsful of pea-size coal into the fire, making the serene glow of the furnace erupt into roaring flames. I remember the thrill of seeing the boiler room glow red-yellow from it. The supers were not always so accommodating and would often chase our noisy bunch out of the alleys.

When you think about it, it was remarkable that, as small children, we were able to be on our own without adult supervision or protection. Since we were close to home, we always felt safe because we could yell up to call someone's mom to the window. Each mother knew the sound of her own offspring.

"Ma-a! Throw me down a penny for candy!"

"Ma-a! A nickel for a Dixie Cup!"

"Ma-a! Can I play in Joseph's house? It's not dark yet!"

The appropriate mother would pop her head out of the window and yell down her answer. Small change wrapped in a scrap of paper would land on the pavement with a dull *thwack*, loose change with a *tinkle*. Some enterprising mother dropped snacks in a paper bag.

Communications went both ways. A mother would call down to her son Martin, "Go to DiNofrio's on the corner and get two pounds onions and three cents soup greens. Tell him it's for Mrs. Goldfarb."

The alleyways also provided a stage for itinerant minstrels. Violinists in rags serenaded us with solos. Arias from Puccini operas were sung by desperate men for the few coins that cascaded from the windows.

Gwen, Howard, and Eleanor, 1920s

After my initial arrival into their world, my sisters, Gwen and Eleanor, treated me like a new doll. Gwen was thirteen and Eleanor was ten. I guess after a while I became a drag. Being a

Sisters Gwen and Eleanor, flanking Howard

picky eater, and not having much of an appetite, often I would refuse to eat. Commercial baby food was either not available or beyond our budget, so all the vegetables had to be manually put through a sieve, which was time-consuming. To have the end result of all that extensive processing, my refusing to eat did not always go over well with my sisters, who prepped my food. Despite all this, they kept me.

The mood for most adults was dour while the country waited for promised reforms. Mom was physically not well, suffering from gall bladder and other health problems. Pop was out of work, since there were no buildings being erected in the city during the Depression. His plumbing chums would come to visit, smoking and kibitzing about the conditions that existed.

But we were all poor as church mice, and the Great Depression was influencing all aspects of life. I remember the breadline in the street. People waited for handouts of day-old bread at Pechter's bakery. They knocked on our door, begging for food. But we were in no position to be of any help.

I LIVED IN MY OWN WORLD. Like the rest of kids in the neighborhood, I ran around the pavement like a banshee. I had real and imaginary friends. My imaginary ones were always available and usually more interesting than the real ones.

Cowboys and aviators occupied my thoughts and provided me the opportunity for one-way conversations. Wiley Post, Tom Mix, Lucky Lindy, Buck Jones, and their planes or horses were my companions. Every kid had a six-gun and an airplane, which brought throngs of kids to the street, pointing and gaping. I could mimic an airplane engine, or the sound of a pistol shot, with the best of them.

By the time I was ready for school, the family had moved to Eastburn Avenue in the Bronx. I found out years later that the author E. L. Doctorow had lived on the same street as we did at the time. Once again, we were on the top floor of a five-story walk-up.

My grandmother, whom I called "Bubbie," lived on the same

floor with Evelyn, Frances, Jonny, Eva, and Sarah. My uncle Jack was married to my aunt Fannie, and they had a son, Charlie, who was eight days older than I. But they lived elsewhere in the Bronx, Jack being the superintendent of an apartment building.

My school was P.S. 70, a short walk from our home. I loved it. My teachers were, in the main, happy to have jobs in the Great Depression and able to bring rays of hope and joy to the children of parents trying to put food on the table during those poverty-stricken years.

In later years, the Bronx Expressway was to scar the neighborhood next to my old school with its noise and the stench emitted by endless streams of traffic crawling in both directions on a road designed to carry a fraction of the load it now carried twenty-four hours a day.

When I was about six or seven, my family moved to the west side of the Grand Concourse, to 174th Street. I was still able to attend P.S. 70 but needed to be escorted by a parent to cross the Concourse.

Although neither of my parents had an education past sixth grade, they closely followed the rise of Hitler in Germany and, later, the Japanese invasion of China. They discussed German anti-Semitism and the brutality of the Japanese. We scrupulously boycotted German and Japanese goods.

My parents were pro-labor and basically Socialist in orientation. The family argued politics, attended the May Day parades, never crossed a picket line, and listened to street corner rallies, quite common at the time in the Bronx. To this day, I'm a proud liberal and prize the logic associated with providing a helping hand to those less fortunate. Tough love, my foot!

It was at one of those rallies that I met Ignatious Lawlor, a man who was to become my brother-in-law. He was a speaker on the street corner of 170th Street. We called him "Bruce."

Bruce had been an electrical engineering student at City College and was later to be responsible for influencing my choice of vocation. Gwen married him in 1935.

Bruce and Gwen, c. 1936

Chapter 3

Peritonitis

IT WAS DURING THE NIGHT, SOMETIME when I was seven, that the abdominal pain that had continued on and off for several days became intolerable.

My mother called Dr. Livingstone, our family doctor, who arrived on a pre-dawn fifty-cent house call, climbing the five flights with his black medical bag. The pain had subsided by the time he arrived. But he examined me, poking my abdomen, taking my temperature, and listening to my heart. When he finished, he tucked his stethoscope back into the black bag and asked my mother, "Have you ever lost a five-dollar bill?"

She owned up that she had.

"Well, take a cab down New York Hospital, and let them

Howard at 6, before peritonitis

look at your son." His face was grave enough to convince Mom. She dressed me, and we were in the ER as the sun came up.

I was soon strapped onto a table, surrounded by several masked people, as a rubber cone was placed over my nose and the ether did its job. I faded into la-la-land. The smell of the rubber cone and ether would haunt my dreams until I was way past puberty.

I woke up frightened and fuzzy, not knowing where I was. The room was darkened by drawn window blinds, and a nurse approached my bed.

I was scared witless as she lifted my blanket and called out,

"He's removed the dressing!" A second nurse ran to my beside and assisted as they repaired the damage I'd done.

Sleep overcame me. I lost track of time, waking up in different rooms with many beds, a ward, occupied by other boys and some men.

As I scanned the ward with blurred vision, I saw five or six figures in black, carrying musical instruments, enter the room. They set up music stand in a corner and commenced to loudly sing, "Brighten the Corners, Where You Are," a hymn accompanied by trumpets and snare drums. I was scared to the point of shaking and didn't stop until they had gathered their instruments and left the ward to brighten the corners for some other helpless audience. Only much later did I find out they were a Salvation Army group.

For several days while at the hospital, I awoke to face liquid meals, a vile beef bouillon, fruit juices, and Jell-O. Between snoozes, I remember talking to members of my family. I didn't know that they had come down to see me for the last time. I had peritonitis, an inflammation of the peritoneum caused, in my case, by the bursting of my appendix, and my condition was critical.

It was 1936; there were no antibiotics then to fight infection. They treated me with transfusions. While cross-matching was known, the Rh Factor had not yet been discovered. Transfusions were performed arm-to-arm between donor and recipient, a nurse squeezing a rubber syringe as it pumped blood from the donor to me.

I had fifteen transfusions during the several weeks I was hospitalized. Donors were family, friends of family, and in one case the father of a boy I had gotten to know in the ward we shared. His name was Eddie. His father told me after he finished donating his blood that, thereafter, I'd have Irish blood flowing in my veins.

Somehow, I improved to the point that I could get out of bed, but I had lost coordination and had to be helped to walk. I was left with loss of balance, learning problems at school, and frequent petit mal attacks. I didn't learn until 1977, when a CAT scan revealed it, that I had experienced brain damage during, or shortly after, my 1936 hospital experience.

Howard post-surgery, c. 1937

Chapter 4

The Store: The Early Years

WHEN I GOT HOME FROM THE HOSPITAL, my mother was burdened with a sick child. I was a shadow of my former self. My legs were like two sticks except for the protrusion of my knees.

Too weak to climb up and down the five flights to our apartment, I spent lots of time on the roof during good weather. Mom and my sisters brought my meals up for me.

Aunt Esther was a kind woman with an unfortunate past. She was illiterate, probably because of dyslexia. My mother had issues with her that I was not privy to, and no empathy for her. Uncle Jack was a wholesale butter and egg merchant, born on the Lower East Side.

It should be noted that Esther and Jack supplied us with some needed groceries during the long haul of family poverty. Jack was a man of few words. He traded in his Dodge every year or two for a new one.

Esther and Jack moved to a Concourse apartment just a couple of blocks from us, and they would take us for a ride many Sunday afternoons if the weather allowed. Usually we ended up at the Kensico Reservoir or Rye Beach.

We knew every bump on the Bronx River and the Saw Mill River Parkways. My aunt would warn us in advance and supply a "whoop-ah" when we encountered one. Sometimes we went with them when they were house-hunting, a project that they pursued for years, never to find one that met their requirements. On one occasion we did a walk-through in a house sporting a swastika flag and a portrait of Der Führer on the mantel piece. It was 1938, and the German Bund packed Madison Square Garden with their crowds.

In order to make life easier for my family, we moved one block east, on 176th Street, into a walk-in apartment facing the street. This enabled me easy access to play on the street with neighborhood kids.

I had a collection of tin soldiers we bought from Woolworth's on 170th Street. This acted as a magnet for me to attract friends in the new neighborhood.

I befriended a boy named Tommy Clearly, who lived in the

same building. His father was a New York City cop. We would sneak into his father's closet and examine his collection of pistols, hidden on a high shelf. He had a sister, Mary, who identified me a Jewish kid. I hadn't thought of myself as that, but it stuck.

I was slowly becoming more adventurous and one day borrowed Mom's clothesline, intending to become a mountain climber. Sporting my brand-new horsehide bomber jacket, purchased from gift money sent as a present of mercy to my family by my aunt Dora, I marched to the Lewis Morris building on the Concourse.

The building backed down a steep cliff extending from the Concourse to Morris Avenue. I tied one end of the clothesline around a tree stump near the top and slid down with the other end of the rope around my waist, then hoisted myself back up, thereby wearing the skin off my jacket. I got chewed out pretty thoroughly when I returned home.

In February of 1938, my niece Judy was born.

Another boy I befriended, George Langberg, lived on our street and also attended P.S. 70, so I had a chum to cross the Grand Concourse with every school day. I guess our moms took turns shlepping us to and from school.

George's father was a furrier, and his family had fled from Vienna during the rise of anti-Semitism, although George had been born here. Our parents became friendly and soon grew interested in starting some kind of business together, perhaps a candy store.

Our mothers had no business experience, although Mom had worked in the Garment District as a young woman. My father's experience was that of a newsboy and an out-of-work plumber. Mom was desperate to free the family from living on Home Relief and was the driving motivation behind this business venture. Pop was less than enthusiastic but was outvoted by her.

After a brief search, both families were attracted to a candy store on East Kingsbridge Road and Valentine Avenue in the Bronx, four stops on the D train north of the 174th Street stop. It was one block east of the Grand Concourse, on a rounded corner flanked by the Poe Park Tavern on the left and Dora's Gown Shop on the right. It faced Poe Park, with the home of Edgar Allan Poe on its property. This took place sometime in 1939. The store owners were the Fellermans, and it was know as Fellerman's.

The property was shaped like a slice of pie, with the entrance at the wide end. The large display window left of the entrance door abutted the tavern. An open service window lay to the right of the entrance, allowing customers to make purchases and enjoy their sodas from the sidewalk.

As you entered the store, a marble soda fountain with four stools were situated to the right, and another two tables sat

The Park Luncheonette

against the left wall. A full-wall magazine rack backed the display window on the left. Deep shelves covered both the left and right wall, past the fountain. Toward the rear of the store, the place had a cigar counter with a closed case humidor, a penny-candy counter, and three public phone booths in a row.

There were deep floor-to-the-metal-ceiling shelves on both walls; each had a rolling ladder fixed to a track at the top.

The store proper ended with the phone booths. Through a triangular-shaped door, you could reach the back room with a trap door in the floor that led to the basement, as well as a double metal sink and a closed toilet room at the apex.

The store was close to a subway entrance as well as a trolley stop. Near a middle-class neighborhood, it was also favorably-situated, with the Concourse; Poe Park with its bandstand for concerts, and recreation areas; and Fordham Road shopping nearby.

My folks borrowed seven hundred dollars from Pop's sister Dora and her husband David Savalle. With this bit of cash and some modest savings, they formed a partnership with the Langbergs, and bought Fellerman's.

Shortly afterward, we moved to 2664 Grand Concourse on the same block as the store.

Howard's parents in front of the luncheonette, c. 1950

My seizures were becoming more frequent and more severe, and the experience at P.S. 46, my new school, came as an unpleasant shock to me. The teaching staff was emotionally much cooler and more punitive with the students. There was a thin, latent anti-Semitic aura in both the teaching staff and the student body.

One day, walking near the school with my friend George Langberg, he was hit with a rock thrown from a group of students shouting anti-Jewish oaths at us. When we later reported his attack to school officials, naming the culprits, we were given short shrift. No action was taken by the school authorities, and thereafter we were bullied without fear of reproach.

While my family got down to the business of learning how to manage a store, I was overjoyed to be surrounded by a plethora of comic books, notebooks, toys, bats, and balls that the store had to offer—not to mention all the ice cream and candy there, too.

There was a toy called HI-LI, consisting of a ball at the end of a long rubber string attached to a wooden paddle similar to a ping-pong racket. The idea was to see how long you could keep on hitting the ball without missing a beat during wild gyrations of your arms and body.

One spring day, I took my HI-LI to Poe Park. I attracted a

crowd of kids watching me as I was playing around with it.

"Where'd you get it?" one kid asked. "Pollack's," I replied, pointing to the store.

"Oh," he said, "you mean Fellerman's."

The kids all ran home to get quarters to buy the gizmo.

This started my life as a shill. Sometimes, I would bring a yo-yo or a top to the park and be innocently playing with the toy, with some skill, drawing kids over to see the action. They, in turn, would run out and buy the same toy. We sold quite a few items this way.

During this time, I became entranced with sun pictures. These consisted of a negative set in front of a sheet of photosensitive paper, all in a cardboard frame. You held the frame up to the sun and waited for a minute or two. A positive image appeared on the paper in a somewhat magenta color. The image didn't last long since no fixative was included, and the paper soon turned a muddy brown. But it was the genesis of my lifelong interest in the photographic image.

The store was a seven-day, dawn-to-midnight venture. Profits were in the pennies—three-cent seltzer, a five-cent (six ounces) soda, a fifteen-cent ice cream soda or malted. You could buy candy for a penny, a Hershey bar for a nickel.

ON SEPTEMBER 16, 1940, AMERICA INSTITUTED the Selective Training and Service Act, the first peacetime conscription in U.S.

history. Military encampments, shipyards, and factories were needed to prepare for the coming face-off with Hitler's war threat.

With this upsurge in building, Pop was able to get plumbing jobs. He and several plumber friends formed a group and went off to work at jobs in the South and Midwest, where army camps were being built. This left Mom, Mrs. Langberg, and my sister Eleanor to manage the store.

On December 7, 1941, the Japanese attack on Pearl Harbor changed everyone's lives. We followed the grim news in the Pacific day by day as the Allies lost ground.

We kept a five-tube Emerson radio in a wooden case behind the cigar counter. After a while, the faint smell of the lacquer permeated the air as the tubes heated up. We listened to a steady flow of war news and analysis while waiting on customers and doing our chores in the store.

We recycled newspapers, metal, and cooking fat for the war effort. Waste fat from cooking got poured into tin cans and brought to the butcher for recycling into glycerine for explosives. Because toothpaste tubes were made of tin, these also were recycled.

Several times a month, sirens would sound after dark, and volunteer air-raid wardens would put on their white helmets and patrol the streets to enforce the blackout rules. Everyone had blackout curtains for their windows at home. Stores went black as we sat inside, waiting for the all-clear sound of the sirens.

As the weeks turned into months, shortages in food brought on rationing. Everyone had ration books and was allowed measured amounts of meats and dairy products. Sugar was also rationed, as well as gasoline and tires. Every car had a sticker on its windshield—A, B, or C—indicating the volume of gasoline allotted to the vehicle by rationing. All cars had the top half of their headlight lenses painted black. Cigarettes were scarce and became a medium of exchange for some people. Black market activities existed quite openly in food, sugar, and cigarettes. Because of shortages of goods, all stores closed a day or two a week. This was a welcome, albeit forced, respite for us.

German U-boats patrolled our coastal waters. Merchant vessels were torpedoed off our shores, and a sticky black oil tar coated the water's edges of our beaches, a mute reminder of the mayhem at sea.

Several customers were ferry pilots flying bombers to Britain over the weekends and returning home on Mondays or Tuesdays. These heroes got cigarettes from our secret stash under the counter.

As a thirteen-year-old boy in wartime America, I was eager to protect our country and defeat our enemies. I followed the newspapers and magazines reporting the war: defeat after defeat in the Pacific Theatre; defeat after defeat in Europe.

The newspapers printed the silhouettes of enemy airplanes. Civilian spotters were on rooftops everywhere on the alert for enemy aircraft. There was no radar yet, but the military did have some acoustical apparatus as warning devices. So I would go up to the roof of my building and check out planes in the air, but nary a Japanese Zero nor Nazi Heinkel was to be found.

Thousand of Japanese families were force into internment camps on the West Coast as the U.S. panicked and turned to cruel acts against innocent people.

The tabloids featured articles describing how to distinguish between the "friendly" Chinese and the "dastardly" Japanese.

I remember reading one supposed fact: The Japanese wore sandals with a thong separating the big toe from the next toe, and this caused the space between those two toes to widen. One had only to get the guy to take off his shoes and socks, so he could be nabbed. This "fact" was a joke courtesy of the *Daily News*.

Eleanor and Mom managed our stock of greeting cards. I was becoming old enough to be a helper in the store. My job was to carry the empty deposit bottles down to the basement and place them in the wooden boxes in which they had been shipped. Additionally, I would manage the magazine rack, removing the previous month's magazines and inserting the new copies. The old copies were returned, and we were reimbursed by the distributors. I was charged with handling the paper for this.

My reward was that I got to read every publication that I found interesting, from *Scientific American* to pulp fiction about World War I and the Spad and Fokker biplanes dogfighting over the trenches. The Red Baron was a foe to fear.

We were also a branch of Womrath's and had a lending library rack in the store. We kept a card file for each person and charged several cents a day for best-selling book-length fiction and nonfiction. Surprisingly, we had no trouble with anyone failing to return borrowed books.

About this time, I created a darkroom in our apartment bathroom. An early ambition of mine was to be a nature photographer. Towards that end, I would take my Kodak box camera to Poe Park and stalk squirrels, hoping for a good shot.

Poe Park was a wonderful oasis in the Bronx. A bandstand stood at its center, and concerts were given during the summer. As kids, we ignored the keep-off-the-grass signs and had great fun outrunning the "parkies" in their brown uniforms, who chased us but never captured anyone.

I loved developing the photos I took at the park and making prints. The emergence of an image in the developer, under the amber light, was always a thrill, even though the scene was often a place that a squirrel had just vacated.

No matter—I was smitten with the entire process, and the

photographic darkroom gave me pleasure for years until the digital age made film obsolete. To this day, the smell of the hypo and developer can send me drifting back to a happy past.

While the advent of digital photography enables anyone to get good snapshots, the software built into the camera ensuring proper exposure and focus, there is, to me, a disappointing aspect to this technology: the sheer volume of pictures that flood the cyberspace. For some people, no event, no matter how inane, is left unphotographed. What to do with the thousands of images of people grinning with a drink in their hand? What to do with the endless close-up shots of people mugging into the lens? Surely, in addition to climate change, this new increase in cloud entropy must have a deleterious effect on our universe, if not our sense of good taste. I wish I knew enough physics to vent my passion on this, so that perhaps the committee in Oslo would award the Nobel Prize to me.

At some point during the early war years, my folks had a falling out with the Langbergs, and we severed the partnership. We were then the sole owners of the business. With the partners no longer there and Pop off working as a plumber, Mom became an entrepreneur. It turned out that she had business skills heretofore unknown.

The shortages of sugar made candy scarce, and candy bars were sold out almost as fast as we could open the boxes in which they were shipped.

Mom acquired a used balance scale and began buying loose candies in bulk. We would weigh out and fill cellophane bags with candy, label the amount in the bag, and staple the bag closed.

She changed ice cream suppliers, too. Then she started serving coffee and buns. We bought Danish pastry and other baked products from Zaro's Bakery, located on our block of stores. Zaro's was to become a prominent name in later years when the sons of the original Zaro family opened bakery shops in Grand Central Station, Pennsylvania Station, and the Port Authority Bus Terminal.

I was a less-than-happy camper, with what would now be called having a learning disability. I knew something was wrong. I couldn't keep up in certain areas, mainly in arithmetic, and had a hard time with the organization of material.

I would forget assignments, and those I did produce were poor and sloppy. My family were not able to help me because they were not educated enough or too busy.

I began to dread school, as I was essentially the only Jewish kid in the class who wasn't cutting it. The teachers didn't help except to scold me. I drew inside myself, and there I would remain for many years.

I ENJOYED LONG WALKS, and the Bronx provided a myriad of interesting places for me to visit. The Bainbridge Public Library was about a half mile from us; it was the science library for the borough and where I first developed an interest in science. I read *Microbe Hunters,* by Paul de Kruif, and books about Galileo and Newton. I remember walking back along Kingsbridge Road laden with books.

I could walk east to Bronx Park and the Botanical Gardens, north to Van Cortland Park, and south to Fordham Road. One of my favorite outings was to Hemlock Grove, a part of Bronx Park where the original native forest was allowed to flourish.

I would sit among the trees and imagine the Native Americans who had walked the trails I now walked on, mesmerized into a solitude broken only by birds and squirrels foraging through the dry oak leaves.

Close to the library I found a shop owned by a man who spoke with a thick foreign accent. He was a glazier who repaired stained-glass artifacts. I had broken the glass of my photo printing frame—a five-by-seven-inch piece of glass. He replaced the plate glass, complete with beveled edges all around, for one dollar.

As I look back at the Bronx I grew up in, I feel that all the joy that I have lived to experience had its genesis in those benign concrete sidewalks, the beautiful parks, and the walk-up apartments that lined its streets.

By 1945, the war was winding down, and I started high

school at DeWitt Clinton, in the North Bronx. In fair weather I walked to school almost every day, past what was then the uptown campus of Hunter College (now Lehman College), where the U.S. Navy had set up a training camp for WAVES. As I passed the wire fence, most mornings there was a formation of trim young women marching out of the mess hall—an ocean of navy blue, all in step, each with a bright orange in one hand.

Chapter 5

High School Years

CLINTON WAS NOT A HAPPY EXPERIENCE FOR ME. I was in a sense defeated by my public school experiences, my frequent seizures, my lackluster performance, and my loneliness—now made worse by being in an all-male school.

I was thoroughly confused, missed classes for no good reason, was isolated by my own problems. I did make some friends through the store: Harvey Altman and Bernie Feirstein. Harvey lived on my block on the Grand Concourse. Bernie worked in our store as a counterman and lived on Bainbridge Avenue. These were my buddies during high school.

Harvey was sort of a cowboy. A Jewish guy from the neighborhood, he spoke with a Western twang like his idol John

Wayne, the movie cowboy. Harvey was into anything that had a motor and moved. He suffered from a leg wound resulting from a motorcycle accident, and was restricted by his parents from this type of vehicle. He was a gun fancier and had an uncle who was a gunsmith with a shop on the second floor of a walk-up on Fordham Road and Webster Avenue.

Bernie was a nice, intelligent guy of few words. He was also into photography but didn't do darkroom work.

Through Harvey, Bernie and I became interested in owning rifles, so we each bought a .22-caliber Mossberg. Harvey had a friend who lived in Parkchester (in the East Bronx) and whose father was a cop. The four of us used to enjoy target shooting at an old railroad station near Parkchester that had been converted into a shooting range. We also went to a police range in Ardsley, New York, for that purpose.

We enjoyed fishing as well at various freshwater ponds and lakes in New York State. We took to hunting woodchucks at various dairy farms in the vicinity of Brewster, New York, and the lower Catskill region, always at the invitation of the farmers, who had a low tolerance for the holes woodchucks dug—a danger to their cows.

At some point in time, Harvey's uncle, Joe Gamsu, the gunsmith, notified him that some World War I .30-06 caliber Enfield rifles were being sold as surplus, and we all bought them at about twenty dollars each. Harvey's uncle converted them to

Howard, as a short order cook, with his friend Bernie in his parents' luncheonette across from Poe Park in the Bronx

sporting use at no cost to us.

And in no time, we were off target shooting and hunting with high-power hardware. We went deer hunting several times, but never got a clear shot at anything on those trips.

One time, I got separated from the group. It was after dark and, having lost my sense of direction, I was trying to find my way back. With no flashlight, I trudged a good long

Howard's parents on the boardwalk

while, until I finally saw the lights of a farmhouse in the distance. In order to get to it, I had to cross a muddy field, my boots sinking ankle deep as I trudged. The weight of the Enfield and my backpack became onerous, and I worked up a good sweat.

Eventually, I got to the farmhouse, and the lady who answered my knock gave me the directions to where we were staying. I detected a suppressed smirk on her face, but she did get me back to the group.

A year or two later, I gave up the guns after an epiphany that one didn't need to carry a gun into the woods to enjoy nature.

Howard's mother, Ethel Pollack, in her 70s

DURING MY FRESHMAN YEAR, I DID LOUSY in Geometry at Clinton and generally got a "D" in most of my other coursework. Later, I did well in Chemistry and Physics. Algebra was difficult for me, but I persevered. Trig was a bright light, as I began to see how math and science were in lockstep. In my junior and senior years, I was allowed to take Analytic Chemistry, a course that needed faculty authorization.

Doc Schwartz ran the Analytic Chemistry course. It was all laboratory work. We were given solutions of dissolved chemicals and had to identify them using various reagents and the rigorous technique drilled into us by the unforgiving Doc Schwartz. One mistake, such as pouring too much of a reagent and spilling the surplus back into the bottle, could get you sent to the toilets to ponder the sin you had just committed.

However hard a taskmaster he could be, he taught us what science was all about. I got an "A" in both his courses, which was a first for me.

A second mentor for me was Gwen's husband Bruce, who showed me stuff like how to wire an electric circuit and how the basic electronic hardware functioned. He introduced me to the works of Norbert Weiner and the book Weiner authored, *Cybernetics*. This was a prelude to my professional career in automatic control systems.

I did not attend my high school graduation, as I had no real feeling of accomplishment.

On the basis of my relationship with Bruce, I chose engineering as my vocation, although I had no idea of what that would mean for my future. I knew it would free me from the store, though, and put an end to a parental supervision that was crippling.

I had no idea of the difference between engineering and physics, or between the engineer and the physicist both in thought and in action.

Armed with this lack of knowledge, I took the entrance exam for City College Engineering School and was confronted with various geometric puzzles that required special interpretations. I walked out after an hour of sweating and hand-wringing.

I signed up for several non-matriculated engineering courses at City, but left after discovering that, in order to matriculate, I would have to swim the length of the indoor pool. Since I have never learned to swim, I chose the land route.

A lawyer friend of Eleanor's who had some clout at NYU arranged an interview for me with an admissions officer, and I was accepted, on probation, to the Engineering School at University Heights in the Bronx, about a mile from my home and the store.

MY SEIZURES WERE BECOMING LESS SEVERE by then and occurring less frequently, shortly after I awoke in the morning. And since I was also on medication that was helping, I decided to learn how to drive.

Harvey was glad to be my instructor, and I drove the gang of four all over New York using my learner's permit and Harvey's tutelage. My parents had treated me to a 1948 Studebaker, the only available car at the time, since the auto industry was still trying to return to prewar production and materials and labor were scarce.

The Studebaker body of that year, designed by Raymond Loewy, was the last word in streamlined elegance, but unfortunately the engineering was far from being on a par with it, and the vehicle was always in the shop for one thing or another that went wrong. I later traded it in for the 1950 model, also a lemon. The company didn't last long after that.

Chapter 6

College Years

I ARRIVED AT THE UNIVERSITY HEIGHTS CAMPUS of NYU as a neophyte in all dimensions, desperately looking for a way out of the store, parental supervision, and a monastic life void of any significant female encounter, especially after DeWitt Clinton, an all-male school.

Alas! University Heights campus was all male—Engineering, Pre-law, Pre-med, Arts students, all men, mostly.

But on the positive side, it was within a mile of the store and my home.

I had chosen the course in Engineering Physics for my degree, a course that would eventually leave me shy of both hands-on engineering skill, without further graduate work, lacking an in-depth grasp of the substance of physics once I had completed my studies and graduated.

FRESHMAN YEAR WAS ALL ABOUT Drafting, Chemistry, ROTC, Calculus, Electrical Circuits, Statics and Dynamics, English, and something called Social Science, all no-nonsense courses except for ROTC, which was required by a state-funded college for at least the freshman and sophomore years, and Social Science.

ROTC required one to carry a surplus Garand rifle for drill and parades, wear a uniform, and show up to pass inspections and perform minor electrical tasks, mostly setting up field telephones. The instructor was a signal corps sergeant.

ROTC proved valuable for the straight "A's" I got to help

Howard , top right, with his physics classmates, and with his beloved professor, Dr. Fritz Rieke, a friend and colleague of Dr. Albert Einstein

my overall average, as did English and Social Science.

Chemistry was given in a huge amphitheater so steep that the head of the person in front of you was visible between your feet. It was almost impossible to avoid seeing his notebook. This was to be a problem in my senior year, when, during an exam in that same room, I was accused of cheating by a proctor located way down on the stage. He came racing up to confront me. I was, of course, innocent. Somehow I convinced him, but the incident was only one of many unpleasant college experiences.

Social Science was a course designed to acquaint us with the visual arts, music, and some history of civilization. This was also a straight "A" course for me, although some returning vets found fault with the instructor. One complained about having to eat Italian cooking during his occupation duty in Italy.

I didn't care for the instructor's opinion that photography was not a true art form, but I kept my mouth shut.

But I was overcome with the initial complexity of college life. I missed classes because I was confused about my program. It was a lonely time.

Stories

Writer's Block

SUNDAY NIGHT I WAS DREAMING. Not my usual dream of being lost and unable to find my way home. In this dream, I'm sitting at my computer, staring at the blank page of my word processor, not able to write. I know that the following morning I will have nothing to read at my writer's group. In my dream, I'm sweating, the frustration is giving me a headache, and a woman's voice says, "Charles, what are you thinking about?"

That again!

"I don't *know!* I can't *think* of anything!" I shout.

She's in tears and leaves the room with a sob.

I've done it again! Even in a dream.

Maybe I should write about being lost—how should I start? My fingers refuse to respond, my thoughts are muddled, the headache becomes worse—it's no use!

Next morning I woke up in a sweat. The room was dark. The only sound came from the humidifier, the hum of its fan blowing moist air into the room. I staggered out of bed and into the kitchen. My mouth was dry.

Later I was sitting at the kitchen table, the coffee machine gurgling away as my headache awaits its product, when my wife came out of the bedroom and saw me sitting at the table.

"Are you okay, dear? What are you thinking about?"

Lost

HE LEAVES HIS WORKPLACE through an exit he has never used before. It's in the city, but the streets are strange to him. He doesn't know where he is, but the sunset is West. People are walking by. He turns three hundred and sixty degrees but finds nothing familiar. A man offers him a cigarette, but he knows he doesn't smoke anymore and asks directions for the train station. The man points to the northeast and he heads in that direction.

He never reaches the station, and no one can help him as he flounders in all directions to find a familiar sight.

Sunlight through the venetian blinds wakes him. He's in a sweat. As his wife comes out of the bathroom, she looks at him and asks, "Did you have another one of those crazy dreams?"

"No," he lies.

Sunday Morning In The Park

I'M LOOKING FOR A TENNIS GAME in Overpeck Park, but the courts are all taken, and a crowd is waiting for the next game to end. A woman and her ten-year-old daughter are hitting a ball against a cement wall. The mother sees me and offers to share the wall. I thank her and buy an ice cream bar for the child, who sits down on a large blanket in the grass.

Classical music from her portable radio fills the air, and a mild breeze elevates page one of the the *New York Times* as we smack a tennis ball back and forth against the wall.

After we work up a sweat, we sit on the blanket and do the crossword puzzle, while the child tells me about her oldest sister, who has stolen some silverware from home and taken it to her college in Colorado. She tells me about her other sister too; she has three altogether.

I tell her that's not really "stealing." She looks at me with wrinkled brow while her mother and I find that we are both going through difficult and complicated divorce procedures. I tell them about my son and daughter living in Rochester, how some weekends they visit me, traveling by Greyhound bus, and about my concerns regarding the New York Port Authority Bus Terminal, because of the crime that takes place there, even as I wait for them.

The little girl's mother introduces herself as Arlene, and I introduce myself as Howard. We exchange phone numbers.

Late afternoon, after I return from the park to my apartment, I find myself thinking about the singles group I'm affiliated with, and how I am expected to be there that evening. For the first time, I wonder if I really have to be there, since I'm overcome by the presence of this beautiful and pleasant woman I've just met that morning.

I spend a lot of time working up the nerve to ask her out. I manage to work up the courage to call her and asked if she would be interested in going out together for some hamburgers.

My heart rises into my throat when she tells me she doesn't eat hamburgers, but then she adds, "Why don't you have yours, and come over to my place later—that is, if you can stand a house full of kids."

And that's the way it all started.

A Sunny Day In Rome

IT'S OUR HONEYMOON. We are in Rome. It's August 1979, and it's hot. Many of the shops are *chiusa*, their owners off to someplace cool.

Arl and I are in the ancient Jewish ghetto, pointing our cameras at the sign in Italian telling the history of the ghetto. It's attached to the second story of a very old building. There are a few people looking out their windows at us as we take pictures.

I am wearing shorts and carrying a shoulder bag around my left shoulder and a thirty-five-millimeter camera in my hand, when suddenly the bag is snatched, and I'm being pulled along the cobblestones on my knees and elbows. Finally the strap breaks and I call out, "I've been hit!" Arl turns, is shocked to see me on the ground, and helps me up. As I stagger to become upright, I see the rear of a small black car with the faces of two men watching me as I stand up. Then they zoom away.

A lady with a concerned look on her face calls out to us from her window. In Italian, she tells us there are police at the end of the next block. We walk to towards the corner, I marching with bloody knees and elbows. There's a car with two *carabiniere*, in uniform, sitting with machine guns on their laps. They don't understand English. Arl tries to explain in Spanish. Finally we are directed to a building several block away; we head toward it.

The entrance is protected by several armed *carabiniere* and a man in civilian clothes, who can speak French. He tells us that we have to report to a police station and directs us to it. We walk.

The police station is ancient. A dank odor permeates the dim interior, and as far as we can ascertain there is only one policeman in the building. He has an old typewriter on his desk and does not speak French or Spanish. Arl answers his questions in Spanish as he types with two fingers. She fills out a paper, answering the questions in Spanish. The policeman finally tells us we have to report to the Polish embassy to get new passports. We get the gist of this and head toward the U.S. embassy, located on the Via Veneto. As we march along, a man sees my bleeding knees and speaks to us in Italian, giving us directions to the embassy.

Wee arrive and were greeted by a black U.S. Marine. I find

it difficult to explain our feelings at that moment. We feel we are at home. We feel safe and grateful to be communicating in English again. I tear up a bit.

We are told by an embassy employee that we are one of dozens of cases of stolen passports that get reported each day at the embassy. We're given directions to a nearby hotel where there's a photographer's studio where passport photos can be made on the spot. We leave the embassy and walked to that hotel.

In the hotel lobby, a person at the desk directs us to the photographer's door. A gentle, elderly man with a beard takes our pictures and presents us with beautiful portraits of ourselves, better than any passport photos I have ever seen. Arl is thrilled by our honeymoon pictures. The price is a bit steep, but the product is excellent.

We return to the embassy, and the clerk informs us that we were directed to the wrong photographer in the hotel lobby. At that point, we don't care. After a trying day, we are tired and eager to get back to our hotel. In a few days, we will be traveling to Venice.

Several months after we return home, we get a package from the Government. Inside we find the stolen, fake leather case that held our passports. No note.

The Ship That Never Sails

WHILE THE WORLD RUMBLES with division and cruelty, Arlene and I live in a tiny spot on the globe, where kindness and consideration reign.

When we began to suffer with the pains and disabilities of age, our children, spread across the country, held six-way conference calls and came up with a plan for us. They decided that we should sell our home at Kings Way and move to a place where we would get the attention we need.

Our daughter, Gail, who lives in Rochester, New York, connected us with social workers here on Cape Cod who dealt with the problems we were facing and provided the help and advice we needed.

The plan was to find a place for independent living, where the help we needed was available. Our children would take care of selling our place at Kings Way, pack us up, and oversee the moving. They would even provide the bridge loan we needed. Our task was to find a place we wanted to be. We settled on a two-bedroom apartment at Thirwood Place.

At Thirwood the average age is somewhere between ninety and one hundred. The female-to-male ratio is ten to one. Just about every interest one could possibly have is addressed here and geared to an aging population. The building and grounds are beautiful. Everyone, including the staff, is friendly, kind, and considerate. In some ways, I feel I'm on a cruise.

On this ship that never sails, all requirements are provided: Five-course dinners, exercise and strength training, a barbershop and beauty parlor, transportation for medical appointments or shopping needs, art classes, movies, a pool table, a singing group, live music, nursing care, computer instruction, even a quaint country store for light breakfasts and lunches, and informal teas.

We've found it is a genteel place that shelters us from turmoil in our old age.

Pixels

I MUST HAVE BEEN ABOUT TEN YEARS OLD when sun pictures entered my life. My parents had bought the candy store on Kingsbridge Road in the Bronx. The store was also a toy and stationery store, and it was stocked with all kinds of interesting things for a boy. After school I explored the shelves loaded with merchandise.

Deep in a drawer filled with pencils and crayons I found the sun pictures. They were in the form of a negative, backed by a piece of sensitized paper and a sheet of cardboard behind the paper. When held up to the sun for about a minute, a positive image was created, temporarily, on the paper. I believe the paper was called "P.O.P.", or printing-out paper, and also was used by professional photographers for proofs. The image so created would fade if left in the light. This experience was the beginning of my lifelong love of photography.

My family lived in an apartment building on the Grand Concourse. It was on the same block as the store, and the apartment consisted of two bedrooms, a living room, a kitchen, and a bathroom. The bathroom was to become my first darkroom.

We sold film in the store, and my parents had a Kodak box camera, which I appropriated. My pictures were mainly of wildlife, or—more precisely—places where wildlife had been a fraction of a second before the shutter clicked. The wildlife was usually squirrels, stray dogs, zoo animals and Petunia, the Wonder Cat, our store pet.

I was inspired by photos in *Life Magazine, National Geographic,* a steady flow of war photos in the newspapers, and such greats as Weegee and Eugene Smith. The store stocked a complete complement of magazines and newspapers, which I read voraciously every day after school. It also carried *Popular Photography* and other photo magazines that introduced me to Ansel Adams, Edward Weston for sheer photographic artistry, and Weegee for the stark journalistic style he was master of. I studied these photo magazines closely and learned what I could about developing and printing photographs.

The Bainbridge Library, a branch of the New York Public Library, was less than a mile from my home, and it was the science library for the Bronx. I found books on photography there, as well as great science books. On Fordham Road, a few blocks from the library, stood Rival Drugs, a store that featured a photography department that sold film, darkroom chemicals, and enlargers, as well as cameras and photo paper. It was there that I spent my allowance every week on all sorts of cans and packages in Kodak Yellow. Film came from our store, but paper and chemicals came from Rival Drugs.

My pictures at first consisted of the tail ends of fleeting animals, trees in Poe Park, bugs, my parents and relatives, and parked cars. Of particular interest to me were the Poe Park squirrels that drank from the water fountains in the park. They were difficult to photograph because they were so quick in their drinking habits. I had many photos of water fountains with absolutely no squirrels to be seen. It was exciting to finish a roll of film and wait for the night to come so that I could develop it in my darkroom. At that time all film was black-and-white except for Kodachrome, which was a slide film. I knew of no amateur color process that one could use at the time.

To use the bathroom as a darkroom, I would hang a black curtain over the window and stuff cloth into the cracks around the door to block the light. I had a lamp with a ruby bulb that allowed me to see, somewhat, in the darkness. If the film was "Verichrome," I could use that lamp to see while I threaded the film into a daylight developing tank. For panchromatic film I had to work in complete darkness. "Verichrome" emulsion was not sensitive to red light, whereas panchromatic emulsion was sensitive to all colors. The panchromatic film was "Super-X," later to be replaced by "Super-XX," the predecessor of "Tri-X." The relative speed for "Verichrome" was 50, and, for Super-X, 100. Roll film consisted of a strip of the sensitized celluloid film, attached by sticky tape at one end to an opaque roll of paper. The side of the paper facing the film was black; the outer side of the paper was red for "Verichrome" and green for Super-X. The exposure numbers were printed on the colored side of the paper so that they were visible through the red celluloid window in the camera back.

To load a daylight tank, one had to strip the film from the paper by tearing it off the sticky tape and then threading the film onto a spiral track of the film tank spool. The spool was then inserted into the cylindrical tank. The light-tight cap was screwed onto the tank so that no light could expose the film. Liquids could be poured in and out of the tank through a hole in the cap because the cap and spool were constructed in such a way that they were a light trap. Light cannot bend around corners, so the developing and fixing solutions could flow in and out with the film safely shielded from any external light. The daylight tank allowed one to process the negatives in daylight, but it had to be loaded in the dark.

Film development was easy once the film was threaded properly and the tank was closed. The developer had to be the right temperature, (usually 68 or 70 degrees F.). You measured the correct amount of fluid and poured it through the spout on the cap of the development tank. Development time was critical, so when time was up, the developer had to be poured out of the tank and shortstop solution poured in. Shortstop halted the development. After the shortstop had been introduced for about a minute, it was poured out and hypo (sodium thiosulphate) was poured in. Usually, the hypo was allowed five to ten minutes to fix the film; then it was poured back into the bottle, because it could be used a few times before it had to be discarded. Running tap water was used to rinse out the hypo, and after about fifteen minutes the tank was opened to reveal the roll of wet negatives. The roll of negatives was washed for an hour on the reel and then removed carefully, sponged off, and hung vertically from a clothespin from one end of the roll.

Usually, it took several hours before the negatives were dry enough to cut from the roll and print. A wooden plank over the bathtub supported the three trays needed for printing the pictures. The left tray was the developer, the center tray held the short stop (dilute acetic acid) needed to stop development, and the third tray contained the hypo. The hypo fixed the image so that it was permanent and could be exposed to white light.

To make the print, light was passed through the negative onto the emulsion side of the photo paper for a period of time. If you exposed it too long, the paper would turn black upon development. Too small an exposure gave an image that was "washed out"; that is, there was no detail in the bright spots. It took skill to estimate the exposure, and there is a wide variation in acceptable exposures. By changing exposures, it's possible to get different effects from the same negative.

At first, I used a printing frame to make the exposures. A printing frame is similar to a picture frame in that there is a glass front and a back to apply pressure. The negative was put right up to the glass with the photo paper sandwiched between the negative and the back. The frame was held up to a lamp and exposed to white light for the estimated "exposure" time. The printing frame only allowed "contact prints," the same size as the negative. As I grew older and my parents saw that photography would be a long-term hobby for me, they bought me an enlarger. This device has a source of light that projects the negative image through some lenses onto the photo paper so that, in principle, pictures of any size can be made.

I didn't realize that, eventually, I had become hooked on the process. The thrill of watching the image come up on the photo paper while it was developing under the red lamp; the smell of the hypo; the measuring and weighing of the chemicals; the magic of the lenses that could take parallel beams of light and bring them to a focused image—these things became permanent parts of my being.

My usurpation of the family bathroom was greeted with less than enthusiasm by family members. This lead me, eventually, to construct darkroom facilities in the basement of the store. There was more room available there but no running water. I had to fill gallon bottles of water from the sink in the back room of the store and carry them down to the basement. Access to the basement was through a trap door in the floor of the back room. There were times when boxes of merchandise or cases of soda got left on the trap door, preventing my exit for a time. The cellar area was dark enough for my work, so dark that at times I couldn't see my hand in front of my face. I can remember one instance when, in complete darkness, I was developing panchromatic film in an open tank when, all at once, I felt extreme pain in my right leg as Petunia, the cat, dug her little claws in and tried to climb up my leg.

I am old now. I have owned many cameras in my time. I have owned remarkable lenses, and the pictures I take now are in color. I no longer process my own work because I live on Cape Cod and the environment doesn't permit the use of photo chemicals, particularly silver compounds that would interfere with septic tank operation. I *would* work in black and white, but it's difficult to find the film and good processing of it.

I use the drug store to develop my film. I scan the negatives and use my computer and computer printer to make the images. Friends and relatives have digital cameras. They hold them up to the subject and view the image on the small screen. If they like the image, they take the shot. Their computer makes the print. It is all so simple and neat. But work using digital cameras and computer printing has not, as yet, produced the quality of wet photography. Color cheats the eye by overpowering it and making ordinary snapshots look stunningly good at times with the richness of the dyes—no particular art or skill required. A black-and-white print by Ansel Adams puts most color work to shame.

There are those times, sometimes just before I drop off to sleep, when I think of the old days and how I miss it: the image slowly forming in the developer, the smell of the hypo, the naive expectancy and feeling of promise that is youth.

Horsing Around

MY FRIEND HARVEY HAD a John Wayne way of speaking. I mean that he had the voice down cold. That slow Western drawl. But it was not only the speech. This Jewish guy from the Bronx took on the entire persona. He loved anything on wheels, although his parents had taken away his motorcycle after he injured himself on it.

He did teach me how to drive and he did introduce me to the sporting world of hunting and fishing. His uncle was a gunsmith and traded in guns as well as fixing and modifying them in his shop over a dress store on East Fordham Road. He was able to get us 30-06 Enfield rifles left over from World War I, which he modified and put sporting sights onto at very little cost to us.

We did a lot of target shooting, and some hunting of woodchucks at various upstate farms, where the farmers invited our efforts to rid them of the varmints.

The sporting life took us to fishing for trout and pan fish in lakes and streams, but I must tell you about the fact that if Harvey was anything, he was a horseman.

In keeping with his John Wayne persona, he was a frequent rider at a stable off Pelham Parkway in the Bronx. He was allowed to ride the fastest horse available there.

One Saturday morning he called me and invited me to join him in riding that afternoon. I told him that I didn't really know how to ride, so he assured me that it was no problem. He would get a horse for me that was trained to follow and would teach me what I had to know, so not to worry. So I agreed.

Getting into the saddle on the grayish mare was not an easy feat. I wasn't comfortable sitting on a seat that moved beneath me, but I managed to stay on the perch as Harvey rode past me on his brown mount. I held the reins loosely as the mare trotted down the bridle path in pursuit of Harvey on his mount. I wasn't comfortable but I hung on, until we came to Pelham Parkway, which crossed the bridle path.

Pelham Parkway is a major artery with traffic flowing in both directions and I watched in quiet horror as Harvey raced across through a hole in the traffic. The mare took off in hot pursuit causing a great squealing of breaks and the honking of horns. I pulled on the reins and the mare froze, causing more horns to join in the chorus. I had to kick her to get her to move and we finally got across to the bridle path, only to find Harvey beating his horse with a twig. The mount had tried to unseat him by racing under a low branch. The mare, seeing this drama taking place did a one-eighty and raced back to the stables, crossing Pelham Parkway, with the horns and the brakes squealing again and me holding on for dear life.

Harvey found me sitting on a wooden bench when he returned. "How'd you make out, partner," he asked.

"A-okay," I said.

And that's the closest I have been to a horse since.

Dr. Livingstone

DR. DAVID LIVINGSTONE WAS a family hero. He was a short man with scraggly red hair and fair skin profuse with freckles. He wore thick lenses in heavy frames, low on his nose, and I remember him as always wearing heavy tweed suits.

The year was 1936. I was seven years old and my family lived on the top floor of a five story walk-up on 174th Street in the Bronx. It was the middle of the night, and I was howling with abdominal pain. My parents were frightened enough to call him.

Livingstone soon arrived toting his black doctor bag, just as the pain miraculously abated. He prodded my abdomen several times, checked my heart and throat, then turned to my parents. "Did you ever lose a five-dollar bill?"

My mother nodded.

"Take a taxi and go to the emergency room of the New York Hospital." He scribbled some notes on a pad and handed it to my mother. She gave him fifty cents for the house call. We were on public assistance and that is what she had, besides the taxi fare.

Thus began the first major trauma of my life. Before the dawn I was on the operating table at the New York Hospital. The diagnosis was peritonitis. Infection of the peritonea caused by a ruptured appendix. I was to flirt with death for several weeks, acquire eleven transfusions of whole blood, and wander in and out of consciousness for five weeks. But that is a whole other story. This one is about Dr. Livingstone.

Fifty cents for a house call. Later on, two dollars for an office visit. For the best part of twenty years, he was our doctor. I often spotted him driving his ancient Chevy on the Grand Concourse, his nose just clearing the steering wheel on his way to another house call.

In March of 1947, a man entered New York City after being infected with smallpox in Mexico. This started the smallpox epidemic that resulted in over six million people being inoculated in New York City during a one month period, more that five million in the two week period immediately after a plea by the mayor for vaccination.

Dr. Livingstone's office was filled with a line of people with exposed arms awaiting inoculation. As one line would file out, the mob in the apartment hallway would form another one and the good doctor, sans tweed jacket would proceed down the line with the inoculations. It should be noted that the method at the time was to pierce the skin several times with a sterile needle and then swab the area with the vaccine. The cost was two dollars, and many people stole away without paying in the turmoil and confusion of the moment. Livingstone never faltered as he slowly marched down the line.

I remember many instances of contact with him, but that day was to me the defining moment in the life of a good man. I can think of no better adjective in English. David Livingstone was a *Mensch*.

Petunia

SHE SHOWED UP IN OUR LUNCHEONETTE and stationary store. I was about fifteen at the time. I picked up a doll's tiny milk bottle and, with its nipple, fed her some milk. After that, she grew tired, found the lap of a stuffed bear, curled herself within its warmth, and promptly fell asleep. From that moment on, she was home and we were her family.

In time, Petunia became pregnant, and we found ourselves the grandparents of a litter of kittens. With little time to tend to them as owners of a store that was open from 6:00 a.m. to midnight, we had to have the vet to do what was necessary, though we regretted it, to assure that Petunia would be a one-time mom. Several of our patrons adopted her children and, we hoped, gave them a home. Petunia adjusted to the reality that she would be the only Pollack child. She saw an opportunity to be useful—

there were jobs to be done, rituals to follow, and she was always ready to help out.

She would wait outside the door of our first-floor apartment until my father came out to go down the street where we had our luncheonette. As soon as he opened the apartment door, she went to work. She led him down the street, past Poe Park, jumped on top of the newspaper stand, then onto the overhead transom and into the Park Luncheonette. This ability was finely honed, a necessity, as she often had to escape the neighborhood dogs that enjoyed chasing her.

At midnight, when we went for a walk, Petunia would be waiting. As we strolled down the Grand Concourse, Petunia pattered ahead of us, waiting patiently for us to catch up to her. It was a nightly ritual. The street was dead quiet at that hour, when we were free from the long hours spent in the store, free to be a family again—a family of mother, father, son and Petunia.

She learned to fend for herself while the rest of us were busy feeding the neighborhood, noting the fact that most of her acquaintances were not aware of their limitations.

Trying to climb trees only to have the local fire department rescue them, that was unacceptable for Petunia, who learned to shimmy up and down the tall trees in Poe Park without a shred of fanfare. When she was lucky enough to capture the occasional bird, she proudly presented it to her human family, who, she figured, needed a happy break from their restaurant chores. For some reason we didn't respond the way she'd hoped we would. Oh, well, she probably thought—I tried, but no family is perfect. Each had a black sheep. In her family, there was a black-and-white cat.

Gastronomically speaking, she had the best of everything. No garbage-can scraps for her. And no food fights between her and fellow felines either. Her people were in the food business! Cans of salmon, tuna fish, abounded. She wouldn't starve like some of her contemporaries.

On the other hand, deaths among those acquaintances abounded in the streets of her Bronx environs. Killing by car was one cause; it broke her heart to witness those scenes. There was, it seemed, little empathy for feline discrimination among the bipeds. In Egypt, I would have been worshipped! she told herself. That's how it goes!

In the end, Petunia herself became a victim of human traffic. She had fallen asleep near the curb in front of her store, exhausted after a long, adventurous day. The owner of the car parked at that very curb decided it was time to go on his way. Unaware of the little cat asleep nearby, he started the car, backed it up. . .and so ended Petunia's life.

Today, a ninety-two year old fellow thinks often about his beloved pet and longs to have her curl up on his lap, purring as he strokes her soft fur. His children, grown now with families of their own, thinking of what would make their dad happy, will soon bring him a little black-and-white kitten to keep him company in his small apartment. They know the name he will choose for it: Pet-two-nia.

Bluebirds

A TRUE STORY

THIS STORY IS FOR THE PRETTIEST

bluebirds of them all:
Brennan, Elana, Hannah, Rebecca, and Ian

Foreword

The incidents and character depicted in this story are all real. The events described were witnessed during the spring, summer, and fall of 2001 and the winter of 2002. The names of characters were made up by the author because he doesn't understand bird or squirrel language, so they couldn't tell him their real names. At times, motivations of animals and bird characters were interpreted with broad artistic license. Grandma and Grandpa are real people who love bluebirds and grandkids.

One day, Grandma and Grandpa were sitting in their living room and looking through the glass sliding doors leading to their deck. The deck was a busy place. Fiona Finch and her husband Ferdinand were eating seeds from the squirrel-proof feeder.

Dora Dove and her husband Dudley were waddling on the floor of the deck, picking up seeds that had fallen from the feeder, and the squirrel pair—Seymour and Sylvia—were scurrying around, also looking for any dropped seeds.

Grampa scratched his chin and said, "I think we should have a birdhouse out there."

"That sounds like an *excellent* idea," Grandma said. So the next day Grandpa bought a book that showed him how to build birdhouses. He studied the book for days and tried to decide which birdhouse to build.

There were houses for owls and houses for wood ducks, houses for chickadees, and houses for swallows and finches, nuthatches, woodpeckers, wrens, bluebirds, and lots of other feathery creatures. Grandpa couldn't make up his mind, so he chose a birdhouse that several different types of birds might want to nest in.

He bought *so* nice pinewood. Then he went into his workshop, which is his garage and, using his saw, cut the wood to just the size the book said. He cut the sides, the back, the roof, and the front of the bird house just like it said to. The front of the birdhouse needed to have a round hole as an entryway for any birds that wanted to get in or out, so he cut a one-and-a-half-inch circle in the front, six and a half inches up from the bottom, following the picture in the book. He wondered how a bird could wiggle through such a small hole!

Grandpa put all the pieces together with screws and nails until he had a birdhouse just like the one in the book. He painted it with a special stain to protect the wood from the weather, and when it was dry, he showed it to Grandma.

"That's a *really nice* birdhouse!" she said. "You ought to make some more just like it for the *grandkiddies!*" So he made more birdhouses, now that he knew how to do it. He sent one to each of the grandchildren and hoped that their parents weren't too busy to hang the birdhouses up on a tree or a wall near their houses.

Grandma and Grandpa also gave a birdhouse to each of their friends. Instead of bringing a cake when they were invited to dinner, they brought a *birdhouse.*

One of Grandma and Grandpa's friends was an artist, so she painted her birdhouse to look like an apartment building. Other friends asked the artist to paint their birdhouses, too.

She made another friend's birdhouse look like an outhouse. Another resembled a Japanese house.

Grandpa didn't think that any birds would want a painted house that looked that fancy, so for his own birdhouse he kept the plain wood color with a coat of stain to preserve it. He hung his plain old birdhouse just outside the sliding doors of his living room.

"Isn't that awfully close to the *house*?" Grandma asked. He didn't know what to tell her. He wasn't sure any birds wanted to be *that* close to his living room, but if they did, he and Grandma would have a wonderful view as the birds made a nest and raised their babies.

Several weeks went by. . .and the birdhouse didn't attract *any birds!*

Grandma and Grandpa got used to the idea that it was empty, and they forgot about it.

Then *Barnaby Bluebird* appeared one day! Grandpa knew

Barnaby was a bluebird because his wings and tail were as blue as the sky on a clear day, his chest was red-brown, and his tummy was white. Nibbling on a bug, he landed on the feeder and spotted the box. The birdhouse seemed like a good place to start a family if he had a wife—a lady bluebird to lay some eggs and sit on them until they hatched.

Barnaby couldn't believe his good luck. He wiggled through the inch-and-a-half hole and checked the box from the inside. It had good drainage and ventilation. The entry hole was small enough to keep out squirrels and big birds. It was just far enough away from some trees, and there was even a feeder close by to perch on. He flew out of the box and perched on the top of the feeder.

If only he had a wife to make a nest.

THE NEXT MORNING THERE WERE *TWO* BLUEBIRDS sitting on top of the feeder. One was Barnaby, the other a lady bluebird named Bertha. Grandpa watched Barnaby fly into the box. Bertha watched him go in, too.

He came out a few seconds later, and Bertha flew in. She stayed on a short time before she flew out and away, leaving poor Barnaby *sitting alone on the feeder!* Poor, poor Barnaby . . .every morning about ten o'clock he came to check the box to see if any other birds had occupied it.

After about a week he brought along a new lady bluebird

named Blossom. She went into the box and stayed for a while. When she came out, *she didn't fly away!* She just flew to the top of the feeder where Barnaby was sitting.

He fed her a bug he found.

Grandma said it looked as if they were kissing when their beaks touched.

Every morning between nine and ten o'clock, Barnaby and Blossom came to check on the birdhouse. First Barnaby climbed the front of the box and squeezed himself into it. Then, after about ten seconds, he flew out and Blossom wiggled through the hole, stayed a few seconds, and reappeared. After doing this a few times, they would fly away.

Grandpa wondered if they were ever going to make a nest in the box. He was ready with a camera and binoculars to take pictures and get a close look at these beautiful birds.

AND THEN, BLOSSOM CAME TO THE BOX ONE DAY WITH a *twig in her mouth.* She tried to get through the hole, but the twig was too big, so she had to drop it. She came back with a smaller twig and went into the box. Every day for a week, Blossom kept putting twigs into the box.

Barnaby was watching from his perch on the feeder. Grandma and Grandpa were happy to see that the bluebird couple were indeed building their nest right there on the deck. Grandpa took some pictures of Barnaby on top of the feeder and of Blossom standing on the birdhouse.

For the next two weeks, Barnaby sat on his perch above the feeder, carefully watching for any enemies that might want to steal the bluebird eggs or attack the baby birds once they hatched.

He was a busy bird indeed. When he wasn't driving other birds away from the box, he was finding food to give Blossom while she sat on the eggs. (It is *very* important for the mother bird to keep the eggs warm by sitting on them—otherwise *they won't hatch*).

Blossom came out of the box every half-hour or so to get a drink or a little food. She also flew to a nearby tree and preened her feathers to make sure they were neat and clean.

ONE DAY GRANDMA AND GRANDPA WERE SITTING in their living room when Clayton Crow came soaring onto the deck to see if he could steal an egg or two. Barnaby appeared from nowhere, beak first, and knocked Clayton *right off the deck!*

Later that same day, Barnaby took on a whole *flock* of birds attacking his nest. There was a loud flapping of wings. Barnaby dove at the birds, looped, rolled, and pecked at them until the entire squadron of eight birds decided that a free meal at the feeder wasn't worth crossing beaks with Bellicose Barnaby, and flew away.

After a couple of weeks more, both Barnaby *and* Blossom

were carrying food into the box. The eggs had hatched, and the little birds needed to be fed! When Barnaby wasn't feeding the young birds, he was guarding the nest. Every morning Grandpa opened the blinds and looked for Barnaby to see if he was on his perch over the feeder. He was always there, ready to drive away other birds and squirrels. Blossom was doing most of the feeding of the young birds, although Barnaby would take time off from his perch to feed them a juicy worm or two.

After about two weeks, *everything suddenly changed!*

One morning in early June, Grandpa had to get up very early to meet a friend for breakfast. As usual, he raised the blinds and looked for Barnaby on the feeder. But Barnaby wasn't there. Neither was Blossom. Grandpa got out his binoculars and looked for them in the trees. He couldn't see any bluebirds at all. They were gone!

Then Grandpa looked at the birdhouse and saw a little head peeking out of the entry hole. It was a baby bluebird named Buster! Grandpa ran to get his camera. He took some pictures of the baby's face sticking through the hole. Then he left for his breakfast date.

When Grandpa got home, later that morning, Grandma told him that she had also seen that baby looking out at the world from the box. The baby wasn't looking out anymore, and both parent bluebirds weren't around either. Grandma and Grandpa looked for them all that day, but it seemed they were gone for good.

The following morning, Seymour Squirrel was back. Some sparrows were eating at the feeder, and some finches were peeking into the box.

Grandpa tapped the box to see if there were any babies still inside. No sound came from the box, so Grandpa took it down and opened it.

Inside was the nest that Blossom had made. She was really a good mom. There weren't any egg shells or dirt of any kind in the nest.

Grandma and Grandpa missed the bluebirds, although now all the other birds were back at the feeder. Grandpa cleaned out the box. He also put some hinges on the side of the box so he could open it and peek in. He hung it back up on the deck. Perhaps later this summer or next spring, he thought, Blossom and Barnaby would come back to nest again.

But three weeks later, whom should Grandpa see on his deck but the two parent birds and a small baby he recognized as Buster! The three birds flew away, and no bluebirds were seen for a while.

THE BLUEBIRDS *DID* RETURN THAT AUGUST and made a second nest in the box. This time Grandpa could look inside and watch the progress as they finished the nest and laid their eggs. He could also watch the babies as they grew strong enough to leave the nest.

He opened the box after several weeks and saw that Blossom had laid four blue eggs the size of grapes. In early September, the fuzzy baby birds left the nest when they were ready.

Here's the way they did it.

One morning Grandma and Grandpa were having breakfast when they heard, coming from the deck, an awful racket of bluebirds calling and flapping their wings. Blossom and Barnaby were flying back and forth from the nest box. A tiny face was poking out of the one-and-a-half-inch hole. The parent birds were urging the youngster to come out into the world. She hesitated and looked like she wanted to go back in. Blossom and Barnaby called to her to come out. Slowly, she poked a wing, then a leg, through the hole. Finally, she plopped down onto the floor of the deck and waddled around for a while. Then the three birds, Barnaby, Blossom, and the baby, Bonita, flew away to the trees flanking the nearby golf course .

Grandpa looked into the nest and saw that the other three babies had already flown away. He and Grandma were very lucky to have been there to see Bonita leaving the nest box.

The winter came with its cold weather, and Grandpa thought the bluebirds would go south where it is warmer. He was very surprised to see them in January! It had been a rather warm winter, so perhaps they'd decided to winter in Cape Cod. They were flocking with a bunch of finches and chickadees. The other birds were attracted by the seeds in the feeder, but the bluebirds came by to check out the nest box. They would sit on the box, enter it, and chase away a pair of chickadees that had shown an interest in the box.

The bluebirds dropped by this way almost every day all winter long. Grandma and Grandpa are waiting for them to nest in the spring and have some more babies.

Photographs

Ponte Vecchio, Florence, 1977

Green Lizard, 1980

Wash Day, Venice, 1983

Black Heron, Fort Myers, Florida, 2006

Arlene, Provincetown, Massachusetts, 1999

The Future, Dennis, Massachusetts, 2009

www.ingramcontent.com/pod-product-compliance
Lightning Source LLC
LaVergne TN
LVHW051011080826
845145LV00009B/2563